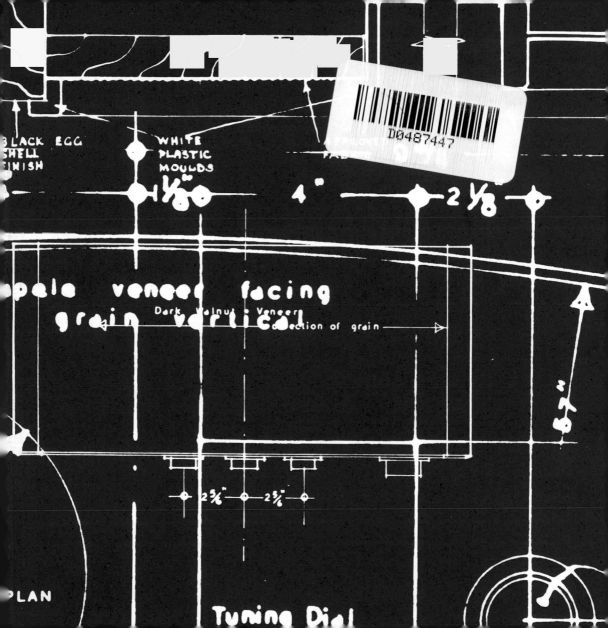

THE
RADIO

THE

RADIO

AN APPRECIATION

AURUM PRESS

DAVID ATTWOOD ⊙ PHOTOGRAPHS BY GUY RYECART

First published in Great Britain 1997 by
Aurum Press Limited, 25 Bedford Avenue,
London WC1B 2AT

A catalogue record for this book
is available from the British Library

ISBN 1 85410 528 0

This book was conceived,
designed and produced by
THE IVY PRESS LIMITED
2/3 St Andrews Place, Lewes,
East Sussex BN7 1UP

Art Director: *Peter Bridgewater*
Commissioning Editor: *Viv Croot*
Managing Editor: *Anne Townley*
Editors: *Graham Smith, Julie Whitaker*
Page layout: *Ron Bryant-Funnell*
Photography: *Guy Ryecart*

Printed and bound in China

Throughout this book the dimensions of
the objects are given in imperial and metric
measurements; height, width and depth are
expressed by H, W and D.

22

15

12

23

15

29

25

11

20

24

24

31

27

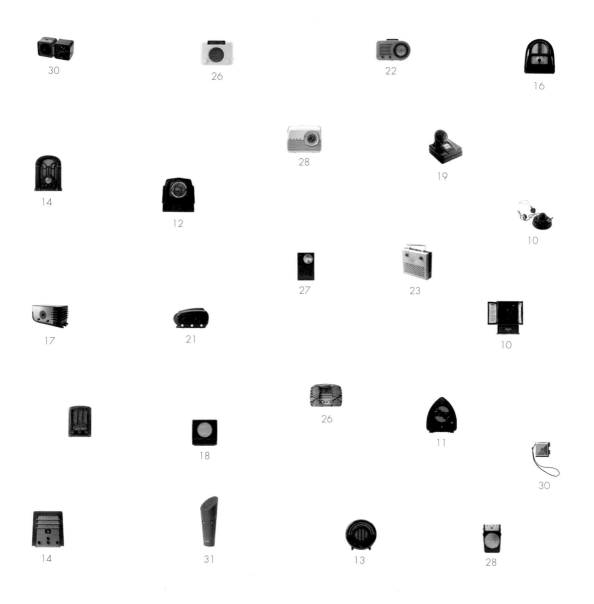

Introduction

Radios have been around, in some form or other, for just over a hundred years, but just what should a radio look like?

The earliest radio transmitters sent Morse code, not news or entertainment, but public interest grew, and keen amateurs began to build their own transmitters and receivers. The advent of broadcasting stations in the US and Britain after World War I meant that millions of people could share the same radio experience.

Crosley G1465
Catalin, 1930s

Saba Oye Oye
ABS plastic, 1996

In the early 1920s, radios really were 'sets' of separate parts: wooden boxes with dials and brass terminals and very often the glowing valves perched on top. There were also large batteries, a separate horn loudspeaker or headphones, and a long wire antenna in the garden. The untidiness of the 'wireless' began a trend to disguise radios as pieces of everyday furniture. The 'smoker's cabinet' set is an early example, but radios also lurked in bookcases and even armchairs. And from the mid-1920s, large and heavy suitcase-style portables were popular for picnics and motor trips. By the 1930s, a self-contained table set (often in a walnut cabinet) was the thing to have. Ornamental speaker grilles echoed the flowing lines of Art

Motorola 49L13Q
Plastic, 1948

Nouveau, but generally, cabinets grew more simple during the 1930s. Bolder Art Deco styles from this period still recall the lost glamour of cinemas and ocean liners.

Setmakers had started using 'designers' to increase the appeal of their products. R. D. Russell worked for Murphy in the 1930s and 1940s; his wooden cabinets were functional but still looked back to Arts and Crafts. Truly modernist designers were often architects first and foremost, inspired by Cubist art and the machine age. In Germany, the Bauhaus art school

Ekco AD76
Bakelite, 1935

was a focus for functional design and architecture.

The use of Bakelite and other plastics in the 1930s soon brought completely new and modern shapes. The Ekco company led the way in Britain, and the now famous

Ekco Princess P63
Cellulose acetate, 1948

Air King
Bakelite, 1933

'round' Ekcos seemed to hail a new and scientific era. Dark Bakelite gave way to other plastics in lighter shades and the vibrant jellybean colours of Catalin were used for many small American sets.

America tooled up for mass production earlier than most of Europe. In the 1930s the USA led the way in market research into what would make consumers buy. Famous names like Walter Dorwin Teague and Raymond Loewy worked in advertising or stage design before making their names as industrial designers, and their sleek 'streamlined' styles for cars and airplanes soon spread to domestic appliances. Skyscrapers, too, provided a powerful image for American designers, as Harold van Doren's Air King radios show.

Even the fantastic glitter of 1950s' American cars rubbed off on radio cabinets. People had leisure time and money to spend, and as TV claimed the family's attention, a radio became more of a personal accessory. Setmakers wooed women buyers with vanity-case and handbag styles.

In the later 1950s German design was again influential. The clean simple lines of Dieter Rams' designs for Braun weren't a mass-market taste at the time, but the

Champion Venus
Acrylic and chrome, 1947

functional look, linked to Japanese technical know-how, led to a more or less international high-tech style by the 1970s.

In Italy, too, the 1950s and 1960s saw a new confidence and belief in 'the good life', reflected in the Brionvega company's stylish radios and TVs.

Emerson 432
Plastic and metal, 1941

Metro-Vick Cosmos
Vulcanite, 1925

The transistor chip, born in the USA in the late1940s, was cheap enough for the mass market by the late 1950s. By the start of the 1960s listening to pop on the 'transistor' spelt teenage rebellion just as much as clothes and haircuts did.

By the late 1970s, hi-fi systems and cassette players had pushed the simple radio into the background, though the style-conscious 1980s brought the 'designer' gadget, and a niche market for matt black models. But by then the functional look was under assault from Post-Modern architects and critics; cult designers plundered past styles and came up with witty anything-goes objects. Today, clockwork and solar-powered sets highlight green concerns, and those old radios, once thrown out as junk, are collectors' items. But they're not just beautiful objects; they give us a glimpse of who we were and how we lived.

Roberts RT1
Covered plywood, 1959

MAHOGANY & EBONITE, 1922, H17 X W11.5 X D9IN / H43 X W29 X D23CM

METRO-VICK 'COSMOS'

S itting in the corner of the living room or hanging on the wall, this was the ultimate economy set. Crystal sets needed no batteries or other power and cost nothing to run. But the downside was having to adjust the 'cat's whisker' (in the glass tube) before programmes could be heard. Not a job for the impatient.

GEC BC2001

T his British set was an early attempt at fitting wireless into the decor. Disguised as a 'smoker's cabinet', the knobs, dials and valves could be hidden away behind double doors while the base concealed the batteries. Headphones completed the outfit, though an extra amplifier and horn loudspeaker could also be added.

VULCANITE, 1925, H4 X W/D6.5IN H11 X W/D17CM

PYE MODEL 25

Pye's fretwork sunburst is one of the most famous symbols in British radio history. This is the first of over a dozen sunburst models from the 1920s and 1930s. Just pleasing decoration maybe – the story goes that it was copied from a cigarette case – but 'new dawn' symbols often had a more serious political message in graphic design of the 1930s.

PHILIPS 930A

By the early 1930s the radio was quite at home in people's living rooms. Cabinets became more upright in shape and often had a style of their own. Philips didn't want anyone to miss the fact that this was a Philips – the speaker grille is a giant version of the company's 'stars' logo. And if wood-effect laminate makes you think of the 1950s (remember Formica?), it's been around longer than that.

BAKELITE, 1932,
H18 X W17.5 X D8IN / H46 X W45 X D20CM

BAKELITE/UREA, 1933,
H12 X W8.5 X D6.5IN / H30 X W22 X D17CM

AIR KING

HAROLD VAN DOREN AND
JOHN G. RIDEOUT

The designer Paul Frankl claimed that modern design owed a lot more to the skyscraper than to the Art Deco styles coming from Europe. Air King in the United States, like Ekco in Britain, was among the first to find a totally new shape for plastic radios. The map too carries a clear message: the world was now a smaller place, with nowhere too distant and exotic to reach from your own living room.

EKCO SH25

J.K. WHITE

Early Bakelite radios weren't so different from wooden ones in shape and finish – you could buy this one in 'mahogany' or 'walnut' effect. The cabinet has Art Deco touches while the 'trees and water' speaker grille is more Art Nouveau. By the 1930s tuning dials had got bigger, and designers began using them as a strong visual feature.

EKCO
AD65

**WELLS
COATES**

In 1932 the architect Wells Coates won a competition to design a new radio cabinet in Bakelite. This was the first of the famous 'round' Ekcos made between 1934 and 1945. Up-to-the-minute black and chrome (see the 1935 AD76 on page 7) seems better suited to its futuristic shape, but Ekco found many people still chose 'walnut' Bakelite. A few round Ekcos were made in other colours (such as green) and are now extremely rare and valuable.

WALNUT, 1934, H17 X W13.5 X D8.5IN / H44 X W34 X D22CM

ATWATER KENT 206

Products of one of the earliest and classiest American radio companies, Atwater Kent sets were always beautifully made. Classical columns and a 'church window' speaker grille give the 206 an architectural look, and collectors often call radios like this 'cathedral' sets.

MURPHY A24
R.D. RUSSELL

Gordon Russell Ltd made high-quality modern furniture, and designer R.D. Russell's work for Murphy moved radio away from the antique look. The severe Arts and Crafts style shocked many at first, but a Murphy ad claimed that 'the longer you look at it, the more you like it!' This seems to have been true, as some proud owners apparently went out and bought new furniture to match.

EKCO AC97
JESSE COLLINS

Like most Bakelite Ekcos, the boldly upright AC97 also came in 'walnut'; but this ultra-modern black version, with what look like eyes, nose and gaping mouth picked out in white, has a real personality. The 'magic eye' tuning indicator – at the top of the tuning scale – was the latest thing in 1936.

AWA RADIOLETTE

Styling trends soon travelled round the world even in the 1930s. Like the Air King, the jellymould shape of this Australian model recalls a world of Deco skyscrapers and cinemas. As well as this ivory colour, it also came in brown, black and pea green.

PHILCO PEOPLE'S SET 444

The American company Philco – which opened a British factory in the 1930s – brought out this fairly basic model after complaints that radio sets were too expensive for the average family. It sold for 6 guineas (£6.30) and about half a million were made. The shape recalls the Volkswagen 'People's Car' of the time, and the 'People's Set' tag certainly helped boost sales.

BAKELITE, 1936, H16 X W12.5 X D9.5IN / H41 X W32 X D24CM

GLASS, CHROME

& WOOD, 1937,

H9 X W16.5 X D8IN

H23 X W42 X D21CM

SPARTON 457X
WALTER DORWIN TEAGUE

Teague, like Raymond Loewy, was a pioneer design consultant in the United States, although Le Corbusier and other European modernists were also an inspiration. This Sparton has the lines of a 1930s apartment block, but it's the amazing blue mirrored surface that makes it a show-stopper.

CATALIN, 1937,
H10 X W7.5 X D5IN / H26 X W19 X D13CM

BAKELITE, 1938,
H9 X W9 X D4.5IN / H23 X W23 X D12CM

EMERSON AU190

Every Catalin set – even those of the same model – is subtly different: the cabinet worker could add dyes to the liquid resin as it was poured into the mould and mix them around to produce unique marbled effects. This 'tombstone'-style model also came in yellow and red.

KLEINEMPFANGER

In the 1930s the German Propaganda Ministry found radio was a good way to promote Nazi policies. Conveniently, this little radio wasn't sensitive enough to pick up foreign stations. It was one of several low-cost Volksempfänger (People's Sets) made by the German radio industry, and over 12 million had been sold by 1939. The symbol of an eagle clasping a swastika can be seen on the front.

PHONOLA 547

LIVIO & PIER GIACOMO CASTIGLIONI & L. CACCIA DOMINIONI

The Phonola's user-friendly style suggests an office telephone – it looks as if you should speak into it rather than listen to it. There were three Castiglioni brothers who became designers – the other, Achille, was later famous for his high-tech furniture.

BAKELITE, 1940s, H5 X W8 X D6IN / H13 X W21 X D15CM

SONORA SONORETTE

Designed in the United States but made in France, the Sonorette's squashy shape does owe something to the bulbous curves of American cars in the days before tail fins were the fashion. It also came in green, white or blue.

TESLA TALISMAN

Is it a train? Is it a spaceship? 1930s streamlining soon spread from buses, planes and locomotives to make all kinds of consumer goods more desirable. The Czech Talisman, with its dashing speed lines and swept-back top fairing, could be the sleekest radio of all.

ADDISON A2A

Catalin – which was too brittle for large cabinets – came into its own in the classic American 'midget' sets. Different-coloured Catalin sections could be combined together – as in this marbled black and white example – to give a huge choice of schemes.

FADA STREAMLINER 1000

Another collectible and highly recognizable American Catalin range that came in many colour combinations; the shape means that it's no surprise the Streamliners were also known as 'Bullet' sets. White Catalin can darken over time to a rich golden colour, which if anything makes it even more attractive.

ACRYLIC & CHROME, 1947, H11.5 X W/D8.5IN / H29 X W/D22CM

CELLULOSE ACETATE, 1948, H7.5 X W8 X D2.5IN / H19 X W20 X D6CM

CHAMPION VENUS

There was growing interest in space and space travel after the war, as the shape and the name of this unique British set seem to show. In fact, clear acrylic had been widely used in wartime aircraft. On a more peaceful note, the way that acrylic reflects light has also made it popular with jewellery designers.

EKCO PRINCESS P63

WELLS COATES

The slim vertical styling of Wells Coates' battery portable gives the lie to the idea that radios didn't look like this until the transistor came along nearly ten years later. And (except perhaps for the colour scheme) the Princess still wouldn't have looked out of place in the 'designer-conscious' 1980s.

WESTINGHOUSE H126 LITTLE JEWEL

Kitchen appliances as well as radios picked up the streamlined style, but the Little Jewel goes one further and actually looks like a baby refrigerator. What's more, if you bought one of their fridges, Westinghouse would give you a free Little Jewel to match.

PLASTIC & METAL, 1948,
H9.5 X W6 X D6IN / H24 X W15 X D15CM

ZENITH TRANS-OCEANIC G500

The story goes that Zenith's chief wanted a high-performance portable to take on his yacht. The first Trans-Oceanic cost over $100 in 1942 but still sold well to people wanting nothing but the best. Many other Trans-Oceanics followed in later decades. Inside the lid is the 'Wave Magnet' antenna, which you could fix to a car or train window for better reception.

LEATHERETTE & PLYWOOD, 1950,
H11 X W17 X D7IN
H28 X W44 X D18CM

KB BM20

LAWRENCE GRIFFIN

This set recalls a 1930s' heater design by Christian Barman. It also came in wildly speckled and mottled Bakelites, but when sober British shoppers wouldn't buy, some stock was painted a darker colour and put back on sale. Other classic 1950s' KBs are the 'toaster'-shaped FB10 and the trend-setting Rhapsody portable.

BAKELITE/UREA, 1950,
H9.5 X W11.5 X D7IN / H24 X W29 X D18CM

BUSH DAC90A

FRANK MIDDLEDITCH

For many people, this is the shape that sums up the look of a postwar British radio. First appearing in 1946 as the DAC90 (which instead has a round knob on the right-hand side), this cabinet design ran almost unaltered until the mid-1950s. This cool cream colour is rarer than the 'walnut' effect.

ULTRA CORONATION TWIN DELUXE

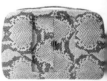

No need to worry about endangered species – the snakeskin covering wasn't the real thing, and neither was the 'crocodile' alternative. Released to mark Queen Elizabeth's coronation, this was clearly the last word in luxury at the time. Ultra called it the 'Twin' because it ran from either batteries or mains power – a popular choice in the early 1950s when batteries didn't last long.

COVERED WOOD, 1953,
H9 X W11.5 X D7IN
H23 X W30 X D18CM

PLASTIC, 1954,
H5 X W3 X D1IN
H13 X W8 X D3CM

REGENCY TR1

The world's first transistor radio wasn't a Sony or other big name. The tiny transistor chip had been invented years earlier, but few then thought of a tiny radio – postwar consumers wanted everything BIG. The Regency didn't sell in huge numbers, but it showed what could be done and encouraged others to follow suit. It was made in black, red, grey and ivory.

PLASTIC, 1954,
H4.5 X W7 X D2IN / H12 X W18 X D5CM

BRAUN EXPORTER
HANS GUGELOT

Gugelot headed industrial design at the Ulm Design School, which inherited the Bauhaus 'form follows function' tradition. Despite that, his Exporter still has American influences. After Dieter Rams joined the company in 1955, he refined Gugelot's ideas to create the totally stripped-down style we associate with the Braun name.

BUSH MB60
DAVID OGLE

Still looking good today, this is the classic British 'rock 'n' roll' radio. It first appeared just as US pop culture took the world by storm, but within a year the transistor boom had made the MB60's valve technology old hat. But with new works and new colour schemes, it went on to sell in huge numbers (mainly as the Bush TR82) well into the 1960s.

SONY TR610

Not the first pocket Sony but the one everyone recognizes. Sony sold nearly half a million of them. A pocket radio with an earpiece put you in a world of your own – just as a Walkman does today. For teenagers, transistors meant freedom and rebellion – especially in Britain, once the 'pirate' radio stations came on the air.

PLASTIC, 1957,
H11 X W13 X D4IN / H28 X W33 X D10CM

ROBERTS RT1

This was the British maker's first transistor
set. The 'champagne' polka-dot leathercloth
(also in blue-and-silver, as well as plain
colours) just about sums up the 1950s' look.
Roberts' radios still sell well today, and their
Revival models are technically up-to-date sets
with styling almost identical to the classic RT1.

STANDARD MICRONIC RUBY SRG430

Radio as personal accessory. Shown actual size, this irresistible jewel-like set came in a silk-lined case with leather carrying pouch. At the time, the Japanese Micronic Ruby set yet another record as the 'smallest radio in the world', and it was made in a variety of models and styles during the course of the 1960s.

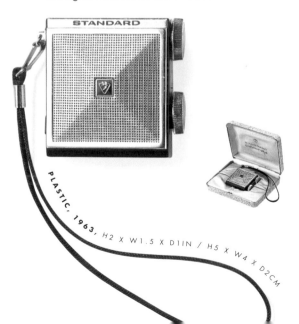

PLASTIC, 1963, H2 X W1.5 X D1IN / H5 X W4 X D2CM

ABS PLASTIC & CHROME, 1964,
H8.5 X W5 X D5IN / H22 X W13 X D13CM

BRIONVEGA TS502

MARCO ZANUSO AND RICHARD SAPPER

A neat Italian high-tech design in two hinged sections, which when open lock cleverly together with a magnet. Closed, it forms a simple box concealing the controls and speaker. You can still buy a similar Brionvega today. Zanuso also designed stylish foam-rubber furniture in the early 1950s; Sapper is famous for the Tizio lamp and Alessi whistling kettle.

PLASTIC & ALUMINIUM, 1970,
H6.5 X W14 X D2.5IN / H17 X W35 X D6CM

SABA OYE OYE
PHILIPPE STARCK

No style victim's home is complete without its Philippe Starck lemon squeezer and toothbrush, and Starck is notorious for his bold new ways with everyday objects. The Saba Oye Oye is one of several recent Starck radios, which have also included models for Alessi.

BANG & OLUFSEN BEOLIT 400
JACOB JENSEN

Bang & Olufsen have long been famous for the restrained Scandinavian styling of their exclusive TVs and hi-fi. The slide-rule-style tuning control on this set added to the high-tech effect, especially in the days before cheap pocket calculators made slide-rules a thing of the past.

ABS PLASTIC, 1996,
H6.5 X W3 X D2IN
H16 X W7 X D5CM

ACKNOWLEDGEMENTS

The author would like to thank members of the
British Vintage Wireless Society for their
invaluable help and advice, and also for loan of
sets for photography as follows:

Carl Glover: page 6 top; 15 right; 18 left; 20;
21; 22 left and right; 25; 31 right

David Read: page 7 top; 9 top; 10 right; 17;
23 left and right; 27 right; 31 left

Gad Sassower (Decadence, London N1):
page 12 right

Enrico Tedeschi: page 19; 27 left; 28 left; 30 left

Gerry Wells (Vintage Wireless Museum, London):
page 7 left; 10 left; 11 left and right; 12 left; 13;
14 left and right; 15 left; 16; 18 right; 24 left and
right; 26 right.

Thanks also to **Steve Harris** of On The Air, Chester.

Endpapers: working drawings for Ferranti radios by
the architect and designer **Christopher Nicholson**
(1947). British Architectural Library, RIBA, London.